First Facts™

Manners

Manners at a Friend's Home

by Terri DeGezelle

Consultant:
Madonna Murphy, PhD, Professor of Education
University of St. Francis, Joliet, Illinois
Author, *Character Education in America's Blue Ribbon Schools*

Capstone
press
Mankato, Minnesota

First Facts is published by Capstone Press
151 Good Counsel Drive, P.O. Box 669, Mankato, Minnesota 56002
www.capstonepress.com

Library of Congress Cataloging-in-Publication Data
DeGezelle, Terri, 1955–
    Manners at a friend's home / by Terri DeGezelle.
        p. cm.—(First facts. Manners)
    Includes bibliographical references and index.
    Contents: Going to a friend's home—Making introductions—Sharing—Friends cooperate—Being polite—Showing respect—Being helpful—Time to go home—Amazing but true!—Hands on: introductions.
    ISBN 0-7368-2643-2 (hardcover)
    1. Etiquette for children and teenagers. 2. Children—Conduct of life. [1. Etiquette. 2. Conduct of life.] I. Title. II. Series.
BJ1857.C5D44 2005
395.1′22—dc22   2003024312

Editorial Credits

Christine Peterson, editor; Juliette Peters, designer; Wanda Winch, photo researcher; Eric Kudalis,
    product planning editor

Photo Credits

Capstone Press/Gem Photo Studio/Dan Delaney, cover (foreground), 4–5, 6–7, 8, 9, 10–11, 12, 13,
    14, 15, 16, 17, 18–19
Corbis/Michael S. Yamashita, 20
Photodisc Inc./PhotoLink/C. Borland, cover (background)

Artistic Effects

Capstone Press/Juliette Peters, 20

1 2 3 4 5 6 09 08 07 06 05 04

Table of Contents

Going to a Friend's Home

Jack **invites** his new friend Max over to visit. Max knocks on the door. Jack opens the door and invites Max inside. Max and Jack use good **manners** when they visit each other. People with good manners are kind and **polite** to others.

! Fun Fact!
In the 1800s, guests often left small printed cards at homes they visited.

Making Introductions

People use good manners when they **introduce** family members to their guests. Jack introduces Max to his parents. Jack says, "I would like you to meet my mom and dad." Max says, "It's nice to meet you."

Fun Fact!
Many people shake hands when they are introduced to others.

Sharing

People use good manners when they share. Jack shares his toys with Max. Max brought a dinosaur to share with Jack. Friends have fun when they share.

8

Friends and guests also share with family members. Jack and Max share the TV with Jack's sister, Sophie. They take turns choosing a program.

Friends Cooperate

People **cooperate** by working together. Jack and Max cooperate when building a model airplane. Jack holds the airplane steady. Max puts a wing on the airplane. Together they finish the model.

! Fun Fact!
International Friendship Day is celebrated each year in August.

Being Polite

Polite people offer their guests something to eat. Jack offers Max a cookie. He pours Max a glass of milk.

Jack and Max are polite when they
eat their cookies. They wipe their
fingers on napkins. They remember
to say "please" and "thank you."

Showing Respect

People show **respect** when they care about others' **belongings**. Jack lets Max see his trophy. Max carefully holds the trophy. He hands it back to Jack.

Guests respect their friend's home. They follow the rules. Guests keep their feet off the furniture. They use quiet voices when reading.

Being Helpful

People use good manners when they help others. Kids can be helpful at a friend's house. Max helps Sophie figure out a puzzle.

Friends are helpful when they put
toys away before going home. They
pick up games and puzzles. They put
books away.

Time to Go Home

Jack and Max use good manners. They share toys and games. They are polite to Jack's family and each other. Max thanks Jack for inviting him to visit. Jack's dad makes sure Max gets home safely.

19

Amazing but True!

In Japan, people take off their shoes before going into someone's home. People take off their shoes to keep their homes clean. Japan's weather is often rainy. Shoes get covered with mud. People take off their shoes so they do not bring mud into the home.

Hands On: Introductions

Introductions help people get to know each other. Try the following activity to practice introductions and learn more about your friends.

What You Need

a group of friends

"Hello."

What You Do

1. Have your friends sit in a circle on the floor.
2. One player begins the game by saying his or her name and something he or she likes. For example, "Hello. My name is Julie and I like dogs."
3. Each player then says his or her name and something he or she enjoys. Each player also repeats what the other players said. For example, "My name is Josh and I like skateboards. Julie likes dogs. Rachel enjoys ballet."
4. The game continues until each player has added his or her name and information to the list.
5. The last player has to remember all the players' names and information.

Glossary

belonging (bee-LONG-ing)—something that someone owns

cooperate (koh-OP-uh-rate)—to work with others and to follow rules

introduce (in-truh-DOOSS)—to tell someone your name or another person's name

invite (in-VITE)—to ask someone to do something or to go somewhere

manners (MAN-urss)—polite behavior

polite (puh-LITE)—having good manners; polite people are kind and respectful.

respect (ri-SPEKT)—the belief in the quality and worth of others, yourself, and your surroundings

Read More

Amos, Janine. *Taking Turns.* Courteous Kids. Milwaukee: Gareth Stevens, 2002.

Nelson, Robin. *Being Fair.* First Step Nonfiction. Minneapolis: Lerner, 2003.

Raatma, Lucia. *Friendliness.* Character Education. Mankato, Minn.: Bridgestone Books, 2000.

Internet Sites

FactHound offers a safe, fun way to find Internet sites related to this book. All of the sites on FactHound have been researched by our staff.

Here's how:
1. Visit *www.facthound.com*
2. Type in this special code **0736826432** for age-appropriate sites. Or enter a search word related to this book for a more general search.
3. Click on **Fetch It** button.

FactHound will fetch the best sites for you!

Index